AROUND
WOODSTOCK
IN OLD PHOTOGRAPHS

WOODSTOCK OXFORD STREET in about 1890, a view north, showing on the right the early eighteenth-century pediment over the Marlborough Arms, removed early in the present century.

AROUND
WOODSTOCK
IN OLD PHOTOGRAPHS

COMPILED BY
JAMES BOND

ALAN SUTTON

Alan Sutton Publishing Limited
Phoenix Mill · Far Thrupp · Stroud · Gloucestershire

First published 1991

British Library Cataloguing in Publication Data

Woodstock in old photographs.
1. Oxfordshire. Woodstock. History
I. Bond, James
942.5'71

ISBN 0-862994-95-0

Typeset in 9/10 Korinna.
Typesetting and origination by
Alan Sutton Publishing Limited.
Printed in Great Britain by
The Bath Press, Avon.

CONTENTS

INTRODUCTION

The photographs in this book cover twenty-two parishes in western central Oxfordshire, extending from the lower slopes of the Cotswolds on the north to the River Thames on the south, and from the River Cherwell on the east to the fringes of Wychwood Forest on the west.

At the centre of this district are its best-known landmarks, the small but ancient market town of Woodstock and the great palace and park of Blenheim. King Henry II founded the borough of New Woodstock in the third quarter of the twelfth century, reputedly to provide accommodation for the many attendants who accompanied him when he visited the palace and park of Woodstock to hunt and to spend time with his mistress, Rosamund de Clifford, the legendary 'Fair Rosamund'. The medieval royal palace is no more, but the park has survived, transformed since 1705 when it was granted by Queen Anne to John Churchill, first Duke of Marlborough, as a symbol of the nation's gratitude for his defeat of the French at the battle of Blenheim. The building of Blenheim Palace and the improvement of the Oxford–Stratford road by turnpiking in 1718 and 1730 gave a new prosperity to the town, which is reflected in its splendid heritage of eighteenth-century houses, coaching inns and public buildings. The fourth Duke of Marlborough provided street lamps in 1768, had trees planted along the main streets of the town, and employed William Chambers, an architect of national standing, to design a new town hall in 1788, while his duchess founded the Almshouses which are still in use today.

By comparison Woodstock's fortunes waned somewhat in the nineteenth century, and there is relatively little Victorian development in the town. Its population began to decline in the 1820s as a result of agricultural depression and limited industrial employment. The Oxford Canal and the main lines of the railways from Oxford to Birmingham and Worcester all missed Woodstock, and it was not until 1890 that a minor branch railway from Kidlington financed by the eighth Duke of Marlborough finally reached the town. Gloving had been the staple industry of the town since the sixteenth century, but although it still employed about 2,000 women and 200 men in Woodstock and the surrounding villages in 1900, most of the gloving firms were small, occupying converted domestic premises; the first purpose-built factory did not appear until the last decade of the nineteenth century. Of the other traditional industries, the bell-foundry established by James Keene in 1626 did not survive the departure of Richard Keene to the east midlands shortly before 1700, while the manufacture of fine polished steel, first recorded in 1598, had died out by 1850. In the present century the development of motor transport has greatly improved Woodstock's accessibility, and encouraged the expansion of mass tourism and commuting, but the traditional functions of the town have continued to decline, the market being abandoned in 1933, the railway being closed in 1954, and the gloving industry dwindling to one single workshop.

Eynsham, the second small town of the area, is of more ancient origin than Woodstock. First named in an Anglo-Saxon Chronicle entry for 571, archaeological investigation has demonstrated a strong early Saxon presence nearby. In 1005 a Benedictine abbey was founded there, and, although abandoned at the time of the Norman Conquest, this later recovered and was the second richest monastic house in Oxfordshire by the time of its suppression in 1539. The town grew up at the gates of the abbey, with a Sunday market first recorded in the 1130s. However, Eynsham lacked any form of local patronage after the Dissolution and failed to develop any distinctive economic base. Its market declined and finally lapsed, although it had a couple of brickworks and a couple of small breweries in the nineteenth century. Like Woodstock it was missed by the main-line railways, although it had a station on the branch line to Witney opened in 1861. Its population too began to decline after 1870, and has only revived in recent decades through the expansion of housing for commuters. The photographs show Eynsham's houses and shops more resembling those of a village than a town; only its street-plan with its open square and diminutive market-hall gives any hint of its former status as a market town.

By contrast Kidlington, though now much the largest settlement in the area, is little more than an overgrown village; indeed, the old centre around the church still has a strongly rural atmosphere. The expansion of Kidlington began only in the late 1920s and 1930s, when the Blenheim estate began to sell land for building on either side of the main Oxford–Banbury road. Rapid growth was encouraged by the availability of cheap land and easy access to Oxford. Kidlington became a byword for the most ugly and dismal form of ribbon development, a reputation which it still finds hard to live down.

The countryside around these three places, pleasant rather than spectacular or dramatic, is still dominated by agriculture, although many of the small family-run mixed farms which appeared after the enclosure of the open fields have in their turn now been superseded by much larger, highly-mechanized agri-businesses. However, the photographers have recorded some lingering survivals of an earlier age, amongst which the working of the Yarnton lot meadows is of particular interest. A special feature of the rural landscape of this part of Oxfordshire is the considerable number of great houses and parks. While Blenheim remains unrivalled in size and grandeur, there are many lesser-known mansions such as Barton Abbey, Rousham House, Glympton Park, Kiddington Hall and Eynsham Hall.

The villages owe much of their character to local building materials. Grey stone predominates towards the Cotswolds. Stonesfield was an important source for the fissile brown limestones used as roofing slates over a wide area north and west of Oxford; here stone had been mined since the seventeenth century and was stacked in the fields to be split by winter frosts before final shaping by hand. This distinctive local industry ceased soon after 1910, although many roofs of Stonesfield slate can still be seen. Further south on the claylands, around Eynsham, Freeland, Hanborough and Combe, brickworks were operating through the eighteenth and nineteenth centuries. The traditional roofing material here was thatch, which is still widespread despite the inroads made by Welsh slate or modern clay-coloured concrete tiles.

Cutting across the visual contrasts which are a result of the use of different local building materials, there were also enormous social contrasts in the nineteenth century between, on the one hand, the 'closed' villages, which remained dominated by the squire and the established church; and on the other hand 'open' villages lacking any single large owner, which were allowed to develop without any firm control and often provided a foothold in the countryside for the otherwise predominantly urban and industrial-based Nonconformist denominations. The legacy of these social distinctions is still strong today. The first group included estate villages like Glympton, owned by a single resident proprietor who provided neatly-designed tied cottages for his own employees but who also followed a strict policy of forbidding the settlement of incomers in order to avoid claims for poor relief; while the second group is typified by Middle Barton, a sprawling unplanned colony of smallholders, craftsmen, tradesmen and labourers which developed rapidly during the nineteenth century.

We are fortunate to have such rich photographic records of this area from the later nineteenth century, not only from the studios of professional cameramen like Henry Taunt of Oxford and Percy Simms and Frank Packer of Chipping Norton, but also from private collections such as that of the Budd family of Woodstock. Their photographs vividly document the landscape and social changes of a countryside in transition, evolving from the relative isolation and self-sufficiency of Victorian rural life through the decline of local industries and services to the onset of the era of the motor-powered tourist and commuter.

SECTION ONE

Landscape and Farming

DRIVING CATTLE past the village green, Combe, on the lane from Alma Grove.

A HORSE-DRAWN REAPER driven by John Floyd, carter, at Swinford Farm, Eynsham, in the 1920s.

A WOODED LANE at Glympton.

A VIEW OVER THE RIVER EVENLODE from Lay's Hill near Hanborough. In the distance is the embankment of the Oxford, Worcester & Wolverhampton Railway and the screen of trees around the edge of Blenheim Park.

WATERING HORSES at Shipton-on-Cherwell, c. 1920.

BROOKE LANE, STONESFIELD, a view south over the Evenlode valley.

A DISTANT VIEW of Stonesfield village from the north-west.

THE POTATO HARVEST, Stonesfield, August 1950.

THE CLAPPER GATE at Wilcote.

SLUICE ON THE RIVER GLYME, Woodstock, c. 1870; the river fed the mill-leat and irrigated the Woodstock Corporation Meadows.

THE ANNUAL AUCTION of the Yarnton lot meadow grass: the party of bidders in the paddock opposite the Grapes Inn, c. 1920. Yarnton West Mead, Oxey Mead and Pixey Mead were held in common between the farmers of Yarnton and Begbroke.

DRAWING THE LOTS for Oxey Mead, Yarnton, 1917. The meadows were held in thirteen lots represented by cherrywood balls, which were drawn at the head of each strip before mowing. The drawing of lots last took place in 1978.

OXEY MEAD, YARNTON. Mowing traditionally took place on successive Mondays in June with hired labour from outside the parish.

Woodstock, Eynsham and Kidlington

OLD WOODSTOCK, view north, showing the elementary school (left) built in 1870. The school closed in 1932 and was used as a village hall until 1974.

OLD WOODSTOCK, the west side of the main road, looking north. As its name suggests, this was the oldest part of the town, settled before King Henry II founded the borough of New Woodstock.

VIEW FROM OLD WOODSTOCK towards the town, c. 1920. The Blenheim Orange Pippin apple was first grown about 1740 in the garden of one of the estate cottages towards the foot of the hill on the right.

OLD WOODSTOCK MANOR HOUSE, formerly known as Praunce's Place after a fourteenth-century owner, Henry Praunce. This name has led to a mistaken belief that the Black Prince was born here. Part of the building dates from c. 1300: note the ornate medieval stone chimney, since restored.

THE CAUSEWAY from Old Woodstock to New Woodstock, showing the mill sluice and pollarded willows.

WOODSTOCK CHRISTMAS MARKET, 1907. The cattle market had been revived in 1869 and moved from the Market Place to the yard behind the Old Angel Inn (now the National Provincial Bank) in 1888. After years of decline it finally ceased in 1933.

WOODSTOCK PARK STREET, C. 1890. Chaucer's House, the large eighteenth-century building at the end of the street, stands on the site of a property held in the early fifteenth century by Sir Thomas Chaucer, courtier and Speaker of the House of Commons.

FLETCHER'S HOUSE, Park Street: Thomas Fletcher leased this site in 1468–9, and his family lived here till the early seventeenth century. The house was rebuilt in about 1615, and the block to the left added in 1795. It is now the headquarters of Oxfordshire Museum Services.

THE GARDENS adjoining the churchyard, with a view to the rear of Garrett's and other houses on the south side of Park Street, with Mr Budd, the Woodstock baker, c. 1920.

WOODSTOCK MARKET PLACE. A view east, with the Town Hall and Bear Hotel, 1900; the open arcaded ground floor of the town hall had recently, in 1897, been enclosed to make further rooms.

WOODSTOCK HIGH STREET. A view west towards the Market Place, c. 1890. The stuccoed building second from the left is Budd's bakery.

WOODSTOCK MARKET PLACE with the staff of the Bear Hotel, c. 1890. The Bear had been an inn at least since the sixteenth century.

WOODSTOCK HIGH STREET, c. 1900, view west showing the house of Whillock, the hairdresser, on the north side, before its demolition.

WOODSTOCK HIGH STREET, south side, looking west, c. 1930.

HARRY BUDD AND C.R. BUDD in the garden of No. 18 High Street, Woodstock home of the family bakery business from about 1850 to 1938.

WOODSTOCK MARKET STREET, a view east in about 1890, showing the former Blandford Arms, which had gone out of business by the First World War; in the background is the Oxford Street shop of Henry Lock, grocer, tea dealer and wine and spirit merchant.

BARTHOLOMEW HOUSE, No. 9 Market Street, c. 1920: one of the oldest in Woodstock, rebuilt c. 1570 by Alderman John Riley, chandler, altered in the seventeenth century, and named from a later owner, Richard Bartholomew, apothecary, who died in 1798.

OXFORD STREET, the shop of George William Smith, grocer, with Mr Newport and the dustcart, c. 1900. The tall houses on the right were built in 1882 by Edmund Webley, a Worcester glovemaster who had recently moved to Woodstock, to house his workers.

THE SOUTHERN ENTRANCE TO THE TOWN OF WOODSTOCK in 1904, with the National School (right), built in 1854, facing Duchess Caroline's Almshouses (left), endowed in 1797.

A WOODSTOCK BACK LANE: Park Lane, a view east, c. 1920.

WOODSTOCK UNION WORKHOUSE, Hensington Road, 1906. The workhouse was built in 1836–7 following the passing of the 1835 Poor Law Amendment Act and was designed to accommodate 300 paupers from thirty-seven parishes. It was demolished in 1969.

NEW ROAD, HENSINGTON, with the railway embankment beyond, c. 1920.

EYNSHAM. ACRE END STREET, looking east in 1906. Note the Railway Inn, dispensing Gibbons' ale. Gibbons' Eynsham Brewery was taken over in 1912 and closed soon afterwards.

THATCHED COTTAGES at Abbey Street corner, looking towards St Leonard's church, Eynsham.

EYNSHAM MARKET HALL, seen here from the church tower, was built in 1701 to house the court house and John Bartholomew's charity school. Its open ground-floor arcade was enclosed as a gaol in the late nineteenth century. In front is the medieval market cross, reinforced with iron strapping by Mr Burden, the local blacksmith, before 1910.

EYNSHAM, THE SQUARE from the south-west in 1906, looking towards H. Field's cycle and motor works. The cross is not yet encased in iron strapping.

NEWLAND STREET, a view north-east from the Mill Street junction, c. 1910. This street was laid out by the Abbot of Eynsham in 1215, as an extension of the older town.

THE MARKET CROSS AND THE SQUARE, Eynsham, a view north-east, c. 1885. Markets were held in the square from about 1140, but lapsed in the seventeenth century, though later revived on a small scale. The Red Lion, in the background, had been an inn since the early seventeenth century, previously known as 'The Angel'.

CHURCH STREET, KIDLINGTON, in the 1930s. This view towards St Mary's church shows the old part of Kidlington still retaining the air of a village, as it does today.

KIDLINGTON HIGH STREET, c. 1930.

THE EARLY YEARS OF KIDLINGTON'S EXPANSION: the Oxford Road, c. 1935, with the garage and Truby's Café.

NEW HOUSES FOR SALE in The Moors, Kidlington.

SECTION THREE
Village Scenes

BLADON, THE OLD MALT HOUSE, C. 1890. This curious building includes some fifteenth-century windows and a doorway, possibly salvaged from the ruins of Woodstock Palace.

CASSINGTON, the village green, September 1916.

COMBE GREEN, 1909: this has been the main focus of Combe since the earlier village in the Evenlode Valley was wiped out by the Black Death.

FREELAND: a new village of the late nineteenth century.

GEESE ON THE POND near Elm Farm, Freeland.

GLYMPTON VILLAGE GREEN, C. 1910; note the stocks beneath the tree on the left.

GLYMPTON, C. 1910: the village was largely rebuilt with new cottages for farm employees by George Henry Barnett, owner of the Glympton Park estate from 1847 to 1871.

THE MEDIEVAL VILLAGE CROSS, Kiddington.

THE BAKERY at Long Hanborough.

MIDDLE BARTON from the Kiddington road. Middle Barton experienced rapid expansion in the nineteenth century as an 'open' village settled by smallholders, craftsmen and traders.

A TERRACE OF THATCHED COTTAGES in Middle Barton.

A CORNER OF NORTH LEIGH.

NORTH LEIGH, a view to the Saxon church tower from the south-west.

STONESFIELD, a view north-west over the higher part of Stocky Bottom.

TACKLEY, eighteenth- and nineteenth-century cottages in Nethercote End, with the King's Arms, first recorded about 1840.

TACKLEY VILLAGE GREEN.

THE BRIDGE ABOVE PARK FARM, Westcote Barton, which was rebuilt in 1868.

THE FORD across the River Dorn, Westcote Barton.

WILCOTE, the seventeenth-century Manor House from the east.

WOOTTON, a general view of the village from the south-east, c. 1870.

WOOTTON, a view of the village and church across the Glyme valley from West End.

WOOTTON, a view of the church with the village school.

HIGH STREET, WOOTTON, a view south from the church.

WOOTTON, showing the corn mill and new bridge of 1840 from Zion Hill.

WOOTTON, Horseshoe Lane, a view to the Three Horseshoes Inn.

A VIEW EAST from near Hill Farm, Yarnton, c. 1920.

A CORNER OF YARNTON with the post office, a view from the east.

SECTION FOUR

Shops and Pubs

THE ROYAL SUN at Begbroke, an inn since the eighteenth century.

THE VILLAGE STORE at Bladon, a converted Blenheim estate cottage, with the shop front built over the front garden. The photograph was taken soon after Percy Maisey had set up business there in the early 1930s.

THE EIGHTEENTH-CENTURY RED LION INN by the village green, Cassington.

INSIDE THE VILLAGE SHOP and post office, Cassington, c. 1950.

COMBE POST OFFICE.

THE NEW INN at Freeland, c. 1900. Built by William Merry in 1842, it was acquired by Morrell's Brewery four years later. In 1974 it was renamed 'The Oxfordshire Yeoman'.

THE KING'S ARMS in Moor Street, Kidlington, 1904. This inn, first recorded in 1817, was built over part of the former Town Green. In the background is Thornbury House, built in the 1760s by Richard Hanwell, son of an Oxford brewer.

THE RED LION, first recorded in 1864, and the Co-operative stores, Kidlington. Both were built on land enclosed from the former common, Kidlington Green.

THE BLACK BULL on the Banbury road, Kidlington, September 1904.

THE ST CUTHBERT'S COMMERCIAL AND FAMILY HOTEL in Kidlington, which operated under the proprietorship of Mr M.J. Thorne in the 1940s.

ST CUTHBERT'S HOTEL, Kidlington, the tea-room.

LONG HANBOROUGH POST OFFICE, a view east towards the George & Dragon.

THE GEORGE & DRAGON, Long Hanborough, an alehouse since the eighteenth century, a view west.

WOODSTOCK HARDWARE STORES, March 1937: a window display promoting Carter's Seeds, with a Coronation banner.

BARRETT'S RESTAURANT in Woodstock: interior view, November 1947. Ernest William Barrett's bakery in Oxford Street operated from about 1900 to 1950.

THE PRINCE OF WALES INN in Woodstock, now No. 11 High Street. In the 1780s this was known as 'The Dog and Duck', was renamed 'The Jolly Farmers' in about 1820, and took the name shown here soon after 1850. It had closed shortly before the First World War.

THE BUTCHER'S SHOP, 49 Oxford Street, Woodstock.

THE VILLAGE SHOP, Wootton, c. 1880.

THE KING'S HEAD, Wootton, first recorded as an inn in the 1930s.

THE THREE HORSESHOES, Wootton, C. 1910; possibly the inn known as 'The Weathercock' in the late eighteenth century, this was converted to a private house in about 1950. Hitchmans were brewers in Chipping Norton, taken over by Hunt Edmunds of Banbury in 1925.

THE GRAPES INN, Oxford Road, Yarnton, c. 1916. This has been an inn at least since the 1750s.

SECTION FIVE

Church, Chapel and School

THE PRIMITIVE METHODIST CHAPEL, Cassington, built in 1870.

ST PETER'S CHURCH, Cassington, was built shortly before 1123, with the upper part of the tower and spire added in 1318.

Begbroke Church.

AN EARLY VIEW of the twelfth-century St Michael's church, Begbroke.

ST MARTIN'S CHURCH, Bladon, c. 1900: this, the ancient parish church of Woodstock, was twice rebuilt in the nineteenth century.

BLADON CHURCH, the interior after its drastic restoration by A.W. Blomfield in 1891.

THE CHURCH OF SS PETER & PAUL and the village school at Church Hanborough.

THE UNITED FREE METHODIST CHAPEL, Combe, built over part of the village green in 1861–3. The occupants of the cottages behind agreed to the use of this site since they were members of the congregation.

ST LAURENCE'S CHURCH, Combe; this view shows the fourteenth- and fifteenth-century interior with its wall paintings. This replaced the older church in the valley, abandoned after the Black Death.

ST LEONARD'S CHURCH, Eynsham, from the Square in April 1906. The town church and market square lay just outside the gates of the great Benedictine abbey, which was destroyed after the Dissolution.

ST MARY'S CHURCH, Freeland, a view from the north in 1901. This typical Gothic Revival church was designed by J.L. Pearson and built in 1869–71 at the expense of the Taunton family of Freeland Lodge. The vicar of Eynsham, who had agreed to the creation of the new parish, later bitterly opposed the high church form of worship used at Freeland.

THE INTERIOR OF FREELAND CHURCH in 1901, with fittings and decoration by Clayton & Bell.

O magnify the LORD
with me, and let us
exalt his name together.

THE INTERIOR OF THE NEW WESLEYAN CHAPEL built in 1895 at Long Hanborough, which replaced an older chapel nearby, later converted to a parish hall.

NORTH LEIGH VICARAGE, rebuilt in the 1720s, with the Saxon church tower behind.

A VIEW OF NORTH LEIGH with the Wesleyan Methodist chapel, rebuilt in 1873.

THE TEMPORARY BUILDING used by the Roman Catholic congregation in Woodstock, c. 1920, before the opening of the present St Hugh's church in Hensington Road in 1934.

ST BARTHOLOMEW'S CHURCH, Yarnton, c. 1885, showing the tower, porch and south chapel, all built in Perpendicular style by Sir Thomas Spencer of Yarnton Manor between 1611 and 1616.

AN UNDATED GROUP, Bladon village school.

BLADON VILLAGE SCHOOL, built with the support of the Duke of Marlborough in 1858, enlarged 1890. This view was taken about 1920.

THE EVACUATION OF MALVERN COLLEGE to Blenheim in 1939–40, when 400 boys and staff used the Great Hall as a refectory and the Library as a dormitory. The Great Court of the palace is cluttered with lorries and temporary huts.

THE NATIONAL SCHOOL in Cassington, built on a site given by the Duke of Marlborough in 1853.

AN INFANTS' SCHOOL GROUP at Eynsham in the 1900s.

WOODSTOCK PRIMARY SCHOOL, 1910.

EYNSHAM INFANTS' SCHOOL, a classroom interior in the 1920s.

WOOTTON VILLAGE SCHOOL, built in 1835–6, with the block on the left added in 1853. This photo dates from about 1900.

SECTION SIX

The Great House

ST PHILIP'S PRIORY, Begbroke, c. 1920. Begbroke House, first built in the seventeenth century, was purchased by the Roman Catholic Servite order in 1896 for use as a noviciate.

BEGBROKE PRIORY, an interior view.

BLENHEIM PALACE from the air, a photo taken after the completion of the Italian garden but before the construction of Duchêne's water terraces in 1925–30.

BLENHEIM PALACE, the formal garden before the east front in about 1900, before its remodelling by Achille Duchêne.

BLENHEIM PALACE, the west front and lawn in c. 1890.

BLENHEIM PARK, an ancient oak by Capability Brown's lake, c. 1890.

BLENHEIM PALACE, the east front and Duchêne's Italian Garden, c. 1915.

BLENHEIM PARK, Capability Brown's lake, with the 8th Duke of Marlborough's boathouse, built in 1888.

BLENHEIM PARK, Capability Brown's cascade, c. 1890.

THE DAIRY at Blenheim Palace.

THE LIBRARY at Blenheim Palace, with potted palms, c. 1890.

COOMBE HOUSE COOMBE. 2

COMBE HOUSE, the former Rectory, with its knot garden, c. 1920. This southern side of the house was rebuilt by Edward Tatham, Lincoln College's rector, in 1812.

EYNSHAM HALL from the south-east, c. 1920. The first house, set in a park enclosed out of Eynsham Heath in 1781, was demolished in about 1905, and replaced by the present hall, designed by Ernest George for Mr J.F. Mason. The gardens were redesigned by Thomas Garner after 1908.

EYNSHAM HALL PARK, the South Lodge as rebuilt in the mid-nineteenth century by Charles Moreing, c. 1920.

THE NEW LAKE AND RUSTIC FOOTBRIDGE in Eynsham Hall Park, made in 1866 for James Mason. The photo dates from about 1920.

GLYMPTON PARK HOUSE, C. 1920. The house was built in the middle of the eighteenth century for Sir Thomas Wheate and altered in 1846 for George Henry Barnett.

THE RUSTIC BRIDGE over the eighteenth-century serpentine lake in Glympton Park, c. 1920.

THE LODGE OF GLYMPTON PARK, C. 1920. Built when William Wheate first enclosed the park in the 1630s, the lodge was altered in 1880.

KIDDINGTON HALL, C. 1920. The house was rebuilt in Italian style by Charles Barry in the mid-nineteenth century, when the orangery (left) was converted to an open loggia.

ROUSHAM, the south front: the house was built for Robert Dormer in the late 1630s, with the battlemented parapet and ogee cupola added by William Kent for James Dormer around 1740.

THE DINING-ROOM in the 1860 extension of Rousham by William St Aubyn, c. 1920.

ROUSHAM, one of the original seventeenth-century staircases, c. 1900.

THE FORMER LIBRARY at Rousham, remodelled in 1764 as a drawing-room, c. 1920.

ROUSHAM the dovecote and seventeenth-century walled gardens, C. 1920, with the church tower behind.

ROUSHAM, the Venus Vale, laid out by William Kent in the 1740s, as it was in about 1900.

SHIPTON-ON-CHERWELL, the long Tudor-style Victorian front of Shipton Manor, c. 1920.

BARTON ABBEY near Steeple Barton, built in the sixteenth century as the manor-house of Sesswells Barton: a view from the west, with the lake in the foreground.

BARTON ABBEY from the south-east, c. 1885. The house had been much altered in the 1850s for Henry Hall, the Oxford brewer.

TACKLEY PARK OR HILL COURT, the main front, c. 1920. The house was much enlarged in the mid-eighteenth century, but demolished in 1959 to be replaced by a modern house.

TACKLEY PARK, the garden front, c. 1920.

TACKLEY, the seventeenth-century Base Court (the present Court Farm) with its gardens, c. 1920.

WILCOTE HOUSE, an ancient structure greatly enlarged in the 1860s by George Devey for Charles Sartoris: the garden front in about 1920.

HORDELEY FARM: Hordeley was a former hamlet of Wootton, largely deserted by about 1600, when the present farmhouse was built by John Gregory, a wealthy grazier. The Gregorys lived at Hordeley for three hundred years, and the house was remodelled by a later John Gregory in 1750.

SECTION SEVEN

People, Events and Entertainment

DONKEY-RIDING at Cassington village feast, 1914.

A SHOOTING-PARTY at High Lodge, autumn 1896. The group includes, in the middle row, Consuelo, Duchess of Marlborough (third from left), HRH the Princess of Wales (fourth left) and HRH the Prince of Wales, later King Edward VII (sixth left), with the 9th Duke of Marlborough in front (second from right).

THE BLENHEIM PALACE FIRE BRIGADE, drawn from estate workers under the command of H. Scroggs, in 1906.

BLENHEIM GATEKEEPER in livery, 1912.

BLENHEIM COACHMAN in livery, 1912.

THE 9TH DUKE OF MARLBOROUGH addresses a political gathering at Blenheim on the tariff question, 23 July 1908.

OFFICERS OF THE OXON & BUCKS LIGHT INFANTRY at Blenheim, 1911.

CHURCH PARADE, Blenheim, 4 June 1911.

COUNTRY DANCING AT BLENHEIM. The coming-out ball for the seventeen-year-old Lady Sarah Spencer-Churchill, eldest daughter of the 10th Duke of Marlborough, 7 July 1939 – the last great social event before the outbreak of the Second World War.

A GARDEN FETE at Blenheim, 1935.

THE EYNSHAM TOWN BAND in the 1860s, with Mr Russell on the drum.

THE DARTS TEAM OF THE SWAN HOTEL, Eynsham, competition cup-winners 1925–6.

THE MEET OF THE HEYTHROP HUNT at Eynsham Hall Park, 31 December 1934.

OXEN YOKED TO A BAKER'S VAN, probably for Eynsham Carnival, some time between the two World Wars.

THE OXFORD ARCHITECTURAL AND HISTORICAL SOCIETY on a visit to the Temple of Echo, Rousham, 1947.

THE EXTERIOR OF THE STERLING CINEMA, Kidlington, opened in the late 1930s.

THE FOYER OF THE STERLING CINEMA, Kidlington, November 1938.

THE INTERIOR OF THE STERLING CINEMA, Kidlington, November 1938.

THE PAISLEY FAMILY in the garden of Wishaw House, Brown's Lane, Woodstock, C. 1891.
Alexander Paisley was a travelling draper.

THE WOODSTOCK TOWN BAND outside Osborne's, C. 1868.

THE WOODSTOCK VOLUNTEER FIRE BRIGADE outside the Town Hall, c. 1900, including Messrs Jardine, Budd, Whillock, E. Banbury, G. Banbury, A. Webley, W. Miles, P.C. Sweet, L. Morgan and B. George.

CHILDREN QUEUEING for their commemorative mugs outside Woodstock town hall after King George V's coronation, 1911. Note the advertisement for 'celebrated Woodstock gloves'.

WOODSTOCK GIRL GUIDES, who gave a dance at Woodstock Town Hall during the First World War and raised over £14 for the Red Cross Society. Back: F. Softe, E. Hughes, E. Pittick, E. Stroud; front: E. Cowell, H. Brooks, M. Cowell, A. Long, D. Bradley.

THE WOODSTOCK CHURCH BELLRINGERS, 1914–18. Back: J. Steele, S. Peake, B. Rose, G. Budd; Front: Mlss Webley, Mrs Clarke, Miss Steele. With so many regular ringers serving at the front, many towers accepted lady ringers for the first time.

GERMAN PRISONERS OF WAR at Woodstock, 1918.

FRED RING, interpreter with PoW working party, Woodstock, July 1918.

JABEZ MORRIS, the Woodstock fishmonger, at the King's Head, c. 1900.

WOODSTOCK STREET FAIR, Market Street, 1925: the last survivor of Woodstock's four ancient fairs, still held annually on the first Tuesday in October.

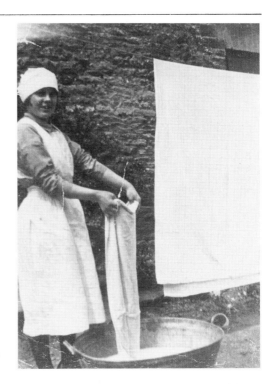

MRS VIOLET HOLLIS at the Bear Hotel, Woodstock: starching in a tin bath.

A MEMORIAL SERVICE PARADE at Woodstock after the death of King George V, 28 January 1936.

CROWDS IN WOODSTOCK HIGH STREET at the celebration of the Coronation of King George VI, 12 May 1937.

OLD WOODSTOCK'S traditional mock mayor-making ceremony was a rowdy parody of the official event in the borough of New Woodstock, held the Sunday after Wootton parish feast (19 September). The gilt macehead is dated 1786.

A GROUP AT THE OLD WOODSTOCK MOCK MAYOR-MAKING. These photographs show the revival of the ceremony in 1954 after a lapse of nearly thirty years.

THE OLD WOODSTOCK MOCK MAYOR traditionally ends up in the River Glyme.

THE GWR STATION STAFF were all enrolled in the Woodstock Corps of the St John Ambulance Brigade. Here they parade before receiving an award from the Duchess of Marlborough on 8 August 1906. Thomas Ashford, seated centre, was the Woodstock stationmaster from the 1890s to 1925.

A GROUP AT WOOTTON FLOWER SHOW, 1924.

SECTION EIGHT

Thames and Transport

SKINNER'S WEIR AND COTTAGE above Pinkhill Lock, Eynsham, 1865. Several generations of Skinners ran the Fish Inn here, until its closure in the late nineteenth century. Joe Skinner (left), the last landlord, was a noted character, who once claimed to have achieved the feat of bringing down forty ducks with a single shot.

EYNSHAM NEW WEIR from the east, c. 1886.

EYNSHAM OLD WEIR, the flashlock replaced by Swinford Lock in 1928.

PINKHILL LOCK from the upstream side, C. 1885. The first pound-lock here was built in 1791.

A PARTY AT PINKHILL LOCK, C. 1890.

A BOATING PARTY near Swinford Bridge, c. 1900.

HEADLEY MATTHEW GARDINER, baker and confectioner of Middle Barton, in the late 1930s.

JOHN FLOYD WITH HIS CART, Mrs Garner and her cousin Ray Floyd at Swinford Cottages, c. 1928.

BRYANT'S STATION CART outside the gate of Woodstock House, c. 1900.

HORSE BUSES outside Woodstock town hall before the First World War.

JAMES TIDMARSH with the Rolls at the Bear Hotel, Woodstock.

THE OLD BRIDGE, Swan Lane, Hanborough.

THE ROAD TO SWINFORD TOLLBRIDGE from Eynsham, looking towards Wytham Hill, c. 1885. Built for Willoughby Bertie, 4th Earl of Abingdon, in 1767–70, this is still a tollbridge today.

JAMES EVANS, toll-collector at Swinford Bridge, c. 1930.

HOLES IN THE ROAD are not exclusively a modern hazard: pipe-laying near the railway bridge at Swinford in the 1920s.

THE OXFORD CANAL at Langford Lane Bridge near Kidlington, a view north to Sparrowgap and Thrupp.

THE OXFORD CANAL below the village church at Shipton-on-Cherwell, with Shipton Bridge.

FAIR ROSAMUND, no. 1473, at Kidlington Station, *c*. 1925. This locomotive worked on the Woodstock branch line from the 1890s to 1935. William Cooke (right), the Kidlington stationmaster, and driver Bill Pomeroy (on the footplate), both served almost as long.

WOODSTOCK RAILWAY STATION, 1908, with the National School.

WOODSTOCK RAILWAY STATION, C. 1900.

FAIR ROSAMUND by Woodstock signal box, with her regular driver, Bill Pomeroy, standing above the wheel, on the extreme right.

SECTION NINE

Industry

THIS APPEARS TO BE CASSINGTON MILL on the River Evenlode, despite its label, c. 1900. The mill ceased work around 1940.

WORKSHOP CLASSES in boot repairing and woodwork for the unemployed, Eynsham, 1933.

BRUCE'S FACTORY, press shop, Eynsham, 1954.

A VIEW WEST FROM BEACON HILL past Swinford Tollbridge to the sugar-beet factory, taken in the 1930s. The beet factory built at Eynsham Wharf in 1927 did not operate for very long, and the premises were taken over for military purposes in 1939–45. A new factory was built on the site in 1984.

THE FARM AND WORKSHOP of Sidney William Smith, carpenter, joiner, wheelwright and undertaker, Kidlington, c. 1905.

NORTH LEIGH WINDMILL, C. 1920. The mill was probably built for Joseph Shepherd, miller and baker, in about 1833.

THE OXFORD & SHIPTON CEMENT WORKS was established at Shipton-on-Cherwell in 1927; it is now part of Blue Circle Industries.

BUNKER'S HILL, Shipton-on-Cherwell, where eighteen houses were built by the Shipton Cement Company for its workers in the late 1920s.

AN OUTWORKER AT HOME in Stonesfield, 1959. Some of the later processes of the Woodstock and Charlbury gloving industry, such as pointing, sewing and buttonholing, were undertaken by these workers in the surrounding villages.

GLOVE MACHINING at R & J Pullman & Sons, 1959. Pullmans, a Godalming firm, built the largest of the Woodstock glove factories, on the Hensington road, in about 1890. It closed in 1966, and is now demolished.

ACKNOWLEDGEMENTS

All of the illustrations in this book are from the Oxfordshire Photographic Archives administered by Oxfordshire County Council's Department of Leisure and Arts, and are reproduced here by permission.

The contribution of the original photographers to this volume is self-evident, and the value of the record which they generated is beyond price; but I would also like to express my thanks to the various donors and lenders and to the past and present curators of the photographic collections used here. Without their interest and care the basis of this book would not have been available.

The original prints or negatives are housed in three repositories, the County Record Office, New Road, Oxford; the Local History collections of the Central Library, Westgate, Oxford; and the headquarters of the County Museum Service at Fletcher's House, Woodstock. The greater proportion of the photographs are from the Budd collection housed in the Record Office; the Taunt and Savage collections housed at Westgate; and the Packer and Simms collections housed at Fletcher's House. Donors or lenders of other photographs reproduced here include Mrs Appleton; Dr Bevan; Mr R. Cullen; Mr F.J. French, Mr P.W.R. Haynes; Mr J.A. Paisley; Mr G. Sanders; Mr P. Spokes; and several others whose names are not available. If I have omitted any due acknowledgement through error on my part, I offer my apologies.

Finally, my thanks are especially due to Evelyn Brown-Grant, who was the first person to draw my attention to the richness of the sources available for the town of Woodstock, only a small proportion of which could be included here; and to Nuala la Vertue, whose assistance with the sources and cheerful efficiency in processing my requests has made my task in making the final selection of photographs so much easier.